Forage

ROSE McLARNEY

PENGUIN POETS

PENGUIN BOOKS

An imprint of Penguin Random House LLC
penguinrandomhouse.com

LIBRARY OF CONGRESS CATALOGING-IN-PUBLICATION DATA
Names: McLarney, Rose, 1982– author.
Title: Forage / Rose McLarney.
Description: First edition. | New York : Penguin Books, [2019] |
Series: Penguin poets
Identifiers: LCCN 2019008922 (print) | LCCN 2019009491 (ebook) |
ISBN 9780143133193 (paperback) | ISBN 9780525504979 (ebook)
Subjects: | BISAC: POETRY / American / General.
Classification: LCC PS3613.C5725 (ebook) | LCC PS3613.C5725 A6 2019 (print) |
DDC 811/.6—dc23
LC record available at https://lccn.loc.gov/2019008922

Printed in the United States of America
1   3   5   7   9   10   8   6   4   2

Set in Fournier MT Std
Interior design by Ginger Legato

Forage

With gratitude to Anton,

and the friends who are why I have continued to write,

and in memory of John Ervin,

who will not see this book published, but never doubted that it would be

CONTENTS

Forage

"WHAT NEED HAVE I FOR LOFTIER SONG TO SING?"

—*Virgil*

In the subdivision, walk looking at the pavement
for spatterings and pits. These from falling plums
no one will pick, not in this setting. In this setting, but
still in the season for fruit. With something to feed on.
Walk looking down so as to know when to look up.

Acorn no more. *Blackberry* blanked out. *Cheetah* cast off.
But if no *almond*, because the young will use language for nature less,

by that logic, no *arousal*, brief surge of blood that cannot continue
but lets lives be conceived. If no *bluebell* because flowers are fleeting,

no *beauty* to begin with for these bodies which wither. If no *cygnet*,
the downy being preceding permanent feathers, then no *childhood*

since those who are sheltered under a wing cannot stay, not the same.
As we might wish *mother*, many children's earliest word, will always

be one they hold in mind, could we let their mouths keep
mistletoe, *minnow*, and *magpie*? Leave a few things intact,

allow the possibility of turning books' pages back
to *lobster*, *leopard*, *lark*, then forward to *last*—to *lasting*—to *live*.

Surrogate, transfer, substitute, ersatz—I set out
to say something of an animal without any of that,
not making it enact some strand of human behavior.

Not the peaceful dove, foreboding crow,
hawk standing for fierceness.

The animal itself. The awareness of nerves
connected to feathers, each quill in the quiver
of skin, inscribing sensation.

What experience is when one is a bird,
does not smell, taste, or wish to stand on the dirt much,
can fly, and swim too, through wind and water
with light bones.

But to put an animal on the page is to still it.
To care for it is to cage it.

Audubon had his birds printed
on the largest pages ever made, at the time.
Yet the birds are contorted, curled and crushed into the corners,
the images always searching out more space, the subjects
too vibrant to be bound in a book.

Who doesn't know Audubon shot the birds he admired,
stuffed them to make models?

The birds I can study are chickens
in the traffic ahead, crammed into crates, stacked on semis.
The waste of their feathers blows back,
and sometimes their whole bodies, in their only
bone-breaking instance of flight. They lie along the roadside,

bodies misshapen by breeding—a great weight on their chests.
It's breast meat, no metaphor.

Though it speaks of us, as must all the animals, live
and on legs like ours, suspended on highway sides,
where habitats are cut in two. Preparing to cross,
many take the same last pose, lifting one tentative paw,
already, off the earth.

When the forest caught fire, the horses
obeyed a fear greater
than what had been bred into them,
broke down the stable, and stampeded
for the opening in the trees,
which was the lake, which was water.

Of course they headed toward
the alternative, liquid,
unlike the material that made
or was burning up the hard world
they had to escape.

It was the 1940s, the bombardment
by Central Powers that started the fire,
in Finland. This is Malaparte's story.

By his account, hundreds of horses
sped through flames, splashed in,
and the second they entered, the lake
froze solid.

Which makes no sense. But never mind
science. The idea stays with us.

Snap—they were suspended,
coated and sealed, suddenly. And singly,
though the herd had entered as a whole.

It could be called tragic because
they were entombed, heads up,
so all winter, soldiers could see
the last shapes failed struggles take.

It could be asserted that the animal face—
flared nostrils, flung mane,
all frozen—is a simplified expression
of human experience.

Something might be said about that war,
what we fight now.

But to merit retelling
there need not be double meaning.
It's hard enough that a horse
had to seek escape and was denied it,
even in decay.

Divisions are hard, how one side does not
see itself in the other, or crystallized,
cast in that clear ice.

The horror of each is its own,
alone. Beyond comparison,

and compassion. The soldiers are said
to have walked among the horses
like a sculpture garden on their smoke breaks.
Casually, to be by themselves,
between the bodies, they went
to light their little fires.

The individual man's flame was too small
to make anything melt.
And not even summer could turn
the sharp edge of this back to water.

The way the cat walked,
stalking—Each step

an extraction of himself,
from the grass, unmoved.

How long I watched,
how I loved

to watch, and how I tried
to make him a little home.

But what is wanted wants
to leg it elsewhere, no matter.

When he was happy,
he was hunting.

He was hunting
the exception to his silence—

that is what he wished to eat.
He would slaughter

his way back to solitude.

Green and red and yellow and yammering,
Carolina parakeets once flashed in the forests.
Flocks so big they blocked out the sun.
Flocks so faithful, when one was hurt, hundreds
would fly back to hover with her.

Which made it fast work to shoot them all.
Which was done, for feathers for hats.
And by farmers whose fields their appetites
had fallen upon. Splitting every apple, every pear,
looking for a kind of seed that wasn't there, yet eating
none. None is how many survive extinction.

There is one print Audubon made of them, paper
tinted tropical colors, in a museum I can go to.
And often I do, seeking brightness, seeking birdsong.
But the image is a warning call, is about waste.
There's a dwindling woodland beyond the window
turned away from, by me in my admiring, by art
finding its ending. Our tending to head back to the dead.

A man should admire rambler roses,
so resilient their vines green what was bare

ground in a single season, then scale up
and overtake trees, strangle whole canopies,

if he can stand his own sort.
And prize redbreast sunfish,

that flash a brilliant blood color. They breed
in streams where native trout cannot now

because the water is too hot, because the shade
was bush-hogged away. Though some

have named the plants that fill in after a clear-cut
pickaninny pines, his is the most tolerant

of species. Which is to say, where such a kind
succeeds, no others can.

There's an old story in the newspaper—about a circus
in 1916, and its elephant. She danced in costume,

kept company with clowns, could play horn
and pitch baseball, and was marching in a parade

when she stopped. Her keeper goaded her.
She struck back. Too hard for his skull to stand.

Then the big show, the crowd convening, the crowd calling
for an execution. The beating, the bullets, the electrocution.

Finally, a crane, a chain that bore her up and didn't break.
Among all the possible material, someone has scavenged

for details to print such as these. It is true, too,
that before her hanging, the elephant had been foraging,

lifting picnickers' fruit rinds from the dirt.
But such sweetness does not make history.

And, from the photo of the mob, there's no picking out
the man who thought only to carry his child to a circus

that day. Before he finds he also holds
the ability to hang a body.

I kept sliding lemon under the skin
and herbs into the openings
of a chicken, its cold countering

the recalled warmth of eggs
in the time when we
collected them fresh

from beneath hens. Our hands,
feather-brushed, found ways
to come near one another.

We took the birds' eggs. We took
their lives too, if raccoons didn't
first, eating the craw full of grain

only and leaving the body
to waste, as the whole of him
does now that he's dead young.

Most waste I can avoid (I'd save hearts,
sauté livers, when we slaughtered).
But not the truth that I have handled

his body, intimately, and other beings'
entrails. And I still make meals.
We were born into a world with predators.

We have lived, from the beginning,
knowing how we were created,
sharp-toothed and hungry.

But not who would have the pleasure
of feeding, when one would feel the pain
of prey. I will serve another chicken,

and I may say its cooked skin is golden,
a kind of exaltation. And the sorrow
will be biting. And birds will keep surviving.

Scavenging insects and flesh from the sick
of their flocks, seeds from sunflowers
and blossoms from rosebushes in reach.

Aquifers are so depleted it would take a great flood
to replenish them, says the radio broadcast.

I am driving from a doctor's appointment, imagining
the millions of us, our failed fields, washed over.

A boat, two of each animal boarding again:
bear and cub, elephant and calf, ape and baby.

But when the reporter says the earth is sinking,
he is not speaking of waves. The soil is falling

to a lower level beneath our feet because groundwater
is gone: a dry drowning.

And the flood fable is the one of male and female, not
mother and child. I can think only of the news

that I may have no children, when there are more
than the world can manage to keep alive.

Must the answer be only the variety
of grief? If not to envy all the irrigated orchards bore,

to sorrow for the trees, sprayed and sterile?

A subdivision's plumbing is a predictable grid,
unlike the errant growth of stalk and vine he's irrigated,
thinks the farmer who sells his water rights, looking ahead.
With the river, it seems nothing moves forward.

Between the mudflats, the fish bones un-swimming.
The banks' dry lips mouthing something about,
My shape made by millions of years filled with—
But the rule of water doctrine is, *First in time, first in right.*

It refers to what was set in writing, not to when
the path of the river was cut. Contracts protect
the claims of impoundment and pipe, price every drop.
There are laws against gathering rain. Too late

for the low basins in the land, the rusted bucket
left out in the field, the fallen log's bowl. And the flower
on damp mornings, that undocumented cup, collecting
another kind of dues?

Men are said to have run moonshine stills. Maybe they weren't
criminal, they were contemplative. Creeks could cool boiling
liquor, but the true fire was in their feelings for the woods.
That's why they spent days wandering up whitewater.

When the women traveled to the next county to buy beer,
it was for conditioning their hair. That was the belief,
though the well water could not have been sweeter
and every curl in that quarter was born lustrous.

If boys drove back roads, bottles open, and swerved
on bridges, if they did sink into rivers, silt bottoms softened
the fall. They were saved by the depth. Deep like the registers
new to their voices when they sang the old ballads.

And some girls who grew up hearing abstain and scrimp,
spurn and scrape by, learned to recall only what fondly wets
the eye. Summer parties in uncut fields. Lingering so long,
before I left, my skirt was drinking dawn dew.

A woman may wake, a coupe from the cocktail
she enjoys each evening left on the counter,

and eat peaches over it, dripping.
While rivers go dry

and the Mississippi—that immensity, crossing
the length of the country—

brings to the ocean such toxicity
they meet in what's known as the dead zone.

Algae *blooms*, consumes oxygen,
suffocates fish, kills even krill.

Blooms. Gardenia and jasmine scent share
the air she breathes in.

Juice runs off her chin, a small stream
that doesn't flow prevailing currents' way,

for which exception is made.
A tributary. If only she knew what tribute,

in return, to pay. And the gulf in her glass,
gathering—if its good could be

of the sweep, of the scale, of the sea.

It's raining and I let myself sit and look
a long time. At water returning, or rather,

that never went away. *Earth today*
has the same amount of water as it did when Christ lived,

I read in a book. A beautiful idea,
so inclusive. And interrupted by news breaking:

Another black American's killing.
This is happening today, so much the same,

a stagnant refrain. And the rivers remain
those that slave songs name. Trade routes

still trafficked, that can't be crossed
to another world, or wash anyone clean.

A river doesn't come from a single spring.
It's side channels, seepage, and sewers, a system

of streams. It's *a participation of waters.*
And in a storm, who can claim she's *just watching?*

How the flow from my gutters goes, to join
the runoff in the public road—

"In this election, arrogance and rancor win with rural white men."

This is for Travis, Levi, Lyman, the end of the gentleness in him
learned from the soft, cupped shape of the coves of home.

Where for every second he spent firing a gun, he'd been silent
days' worth of dawns watching deer, moving lightly as he could

over the earth's surface crackling with fall leaves, among fragilities
to which he paid mind. Where, for any single notion about keeping

to his kind, there were so many minnows to count in the creeks,
bodies of unnamable color moving in an element other than his own.

But for him, the place became a pail whose confines he circles,
the oxygen all breathed up. Where prospects do not brighten

as the landscape is ever more fluorescent lit. He is crowded
into trailers, and with a certain type of men, whose muttered hatreds

headlines and elections declare loudly now. Now, I cannot extract him,
tell of the delicacy with which one boy once drew threads dripping nectar

from the throats of honeysuckle. The truth is, the flowers I remember
him with were plastic. He brought these as gifts to me, and a fledgling

from a nest on the playground at our elementary school. Where he returned
to the polls, where he cast his ballot. The eyes were sealed, yet see-through.

The featherless skin bare against the hands it passed into. The bird died before
the first bell. Maybe I should have been frightened from the very beginning.

Or this should be an elegy for my heart, the understandings, clemencies,
it will no longer hold.

She's stung with resentment like nettle-slapped girl's legs
in summer all year, how many years, not leaving out of here.

So often, mud sucks at her feet saying, *Squandered*. But still
there are a few trout lilies, blossoms down-turned,

heads dropped, faces hidden. Those who don't try to show,
and see something in this dirt. Wildflowers tend to themselves

while all people plant these days are satellite dishes.
Their necks crane in crazy directions to get any shot at the sky,

some signal from far off.

It's cut off, the hotel. From the town
to which there are no sidewalks. The grassy
bit between walled interstates each going
opposite, absolute directions away. The air
outside unopenable windows. The Appalachian
ridges in sight beyond, above the low, base lines
of box stores, but not in reach. The question
How did I ever leave mountains? displaced
by *What's left of here?* in a chain business.
Called that, but link-less. Even fully booked,
a vacant building.

It was isolation of another kind, no roads across
rough terrain, growing up talking to oneself
in an uninfluenced accent, that once let a rural place
keep alive its ways. In the lobby, there's a pamphlet
about the past, folk art. Images to make study of,
here where I'm stuck. A sculpture, an ark, crafted
from scrap wood, populated by pigs and possums.
Not lions and elephants. By locals, not exotics
the carver couldn't, in his time, know. His focus
devoted, defined by hills, tightly framing how far
the eye will go.

Though today too, in a traveler—in rented rooms,
in walls where water sound can only be the brook
of next door's flushing, in departure gates' fluorescent light
where any foliage is faux—sincere feeling arises. An urge
to unseal the sterile, individual package of every lonely
soap and peanut. And the airport shuttle offers a view
of curing tobacco, a traditional crop, or a ruinous one.
But a color that is a glory, in any case. The gold it turns
because it has been cut. So long, the ark was adrift.
Consider the many beasts, the wild beliefs,
it carried forward.

Cattle are a black weight on the light sway of land that was once
prairie. The wind pulls at pasture, wantful; they appear to hold it in place.

Though it was the cattle that ate away the native grasses.
Perhaps the impression is scenic because their necks are bent

with the downward stroke of feeding. I could say the oil derricks
too are feeding, with enormous avian pecks.

Or that they are nodding in assent. Yes, yes, we are allowed
so much. Let us strike, again, the pose of plenty.

Is there time to marry, or at least
to buy a house, plant a maple by the door,
and see it mature? That's what the small
mind asks when someone speaks
about the big picture:

How soon the aquifer underlying
the heartland, water older than the Ice Ages,
will have been pumped dry to irrigate corn,
to feed hogs.

∿

But what about the narrowness of vision
that kept settlers on their land all through
the Dust Bowl? Wasn't it admirable,
how they could not see living elsewhere
and stayed through ten years of storms
while all fertile soil was stripped away?

Of course, there are the broader
human habits. How when we stopped
looking to the sky, the past's reverent pose
of asking for rain, we kept on making
demands from prairie plowed to desert land.
Now irrigators draw water from below,
and we don't drop our heads.

∿

What the Dust Bowl did, mostly,
was make a sweeping statement,
wiping people out. The families who waited
through it were faceless and voiceless, hanging
wet towels over their heads to breathe

through the dust, and so they could not speak.
The earth blurred the fine lines of fences,
drifting feet of itself over post tops
so animals walked above them and away.

Still there is some comfort to be taken
from details: During storms,
people kept close, clustered in one room.
And static electricity sparked
on spikes of barbed wire, highlighting
the boundaries of property.

～o

When every bit of sun
was obscured by the topsoil
of a million wasted acres rising up,
dirt-blinded people reached
for each other in the dark.

And our hands practice the same
spanning gesture across the space
of beds, after every ordinary evening's
blackout falling.

An abandoned mansion,
from the time of Temperance,
what it must have held:

hair bobbed short,
cocktails poured tall,
not just drunkenness

but the double sin
of deception too.
Finally, the house is allowing

itself to fall,
letting down the white walls.
Better to rot outright,

return lot to field,
render lumber down to dirt—
that's the closest to cleanliness,

to righteous, you'll get.
So the sight seems to say.
Or I have come for that answer.

If there is one, to the question
of why be here, anywhere I stand,
anywhere I go.

There is sweat at the back of our necks
seven months out of the year. That's true,

that and an ugly history too. At least,
in the South, the Ice Age never quite came.

I can say that while glaciers scraped the North
clean, here there was only a little winter.

From the warm, deep dirt that remained,
plantations' fruitage grew.

Then their produce, poverty. It's still fresh.
But a great diversity survived,

of animal species, I mean. Our mud is home
to half the mussels on the continent.

Those fine beings filter tainted water.
While the country's sole cave fish swims

unbiased nearby, with no color,
no eye.

In the photos of Sherman's March—no action.
Cameras could not yet capture
subjects in motion. No battles, just battlefields,
landscapes after. Trees, bark blasted off,
burned bridges and barriers overcome.
Broad strokes of blackened fields, sweeping
the eye from the small interjections of fallen fence
and fireplace, standing alone, to disappearing points,
detail broken down in the indiscriminate texture
of rubble and wreck.

For film to register faces, people had to keep still
so long they wore iron neck braces,
not to tremble and blur the picture. Bodies
gun-shot didn't pose such a problem,
and must have piled themselves before the photographer.

But how hopeless the honesty of showing the dead,
when, in a composition, trees can function as a frame,
form a place where tensions are only between background
and fore. And the shattered buildings, the splintered beams—
they thrust up into the shape of branches, growing back.

(after the photographs of George N. Barnard,
photographer for General Sherman)

After the Civil War, painting the American West
was popular because it was not the setting

of either side's tragedy. People thought they wanted
to look at scenes free from the marks of our enemies

and selves. But what man has ever really lusted for
the untouched except in the briefest of moments before

he lays his own hands all over it? Surroundings
that exemplify purity are unsettled, empty.

Eastern architecture's crowded, old walls hold on
to the curios of fondness, along with the clutter of anger.

And, really, isn't the woman most wanted she who remembers
everything, who knows man's faults, and will spoil him still?

Spoil—that's the word used for what builders of houses do
to once-wild landscapes they admire too much to let alone.

Neon signs—why not care for them?
They're historic now. Businesses fail but
the signs' ideas endure far from the actual:

Cleaning nowhere near the wringing
of hands in the laundry. *Repair*
with no wrenches in reach.

These bent and soldered sales pitches,
serenades of gas stations and seedy hotels,
may lack the elegance of antique and artifact.

But there are those who tend to
the flickering of the familiar before it expires.
Who exalt the dullard every day, ignite

a *No* to go against the *Vacancy*,
and live in that kind of light.

THE JEWELS WITH WHICH TO MAKE DO,
THE JEWELS THAT THERE WERE

The woman is wearing, with such style
and intention, only one earring—

she makes the half lost
exquisite. Praise her.

As we praise parks, what's left of wilderness,
and the literature of the diaspora.

Give her the unmatched remainders
of our pairs—one stud, one star, one single hoop,

an actual diamond, antique,
much iridescence, incomplete.

Compliment her further by recalling
that the forest was finest in its first growth—

high canopies hung with the lobes
of a multiplicity of leaves,

chestnuts set in the prongs of pods,
and below, made of birch bark's silver

and mud, a few homes
built where their inhabitants belonged.

Because it means you see what beauty is
here, and what she ought to have:

jewels in a complete set,
presented in a box that opens

to its landscape of velvet, opulent
threads not yet asked to rise back

from the crush of any touch.

(for Tarfia)

I have tried to carry a persimmon home,
to share one fruit. I passed the tree running,

a pursuit which allows no pockets, no bags.
Needs no equipment. No team.

I was many miles away,
and could not clench my fist.

I told myself to hold my hands like good men
every time they choose not

to use their strength.
But a good persimmon

is already halfway to ruin.
A ripe fruit falls,

wrinkled and dark.
Too fragile to bear reaching the ground,

it bursts. Too fragile to bear touch,
the skin of the fruit I gathered

skidded off. Pulp pushed past
my knuckles' best intentions.

Men can be considered good
for what they don't do. How small

of a taken action could be a saving
grace then? I tried again, another day,

dropping a persimmon in the emptiness
between my breasts.

Home, undressed,
there was only a sweaty smear

no man could find sensuous.
Some things are best

enjoyed alone. Some things can only be
enjoyed alone.

And so, this morning, I eat right
on the roadside, picking grit from fruit's soft insides.

Across town, a man I love sleeps.
Around the world, the hungry and sleepless.

Here, my fingers so sugared
I can't suck them clean.

Ruskin acclaims valleys not wide,
forests of no extent, because they are
of England, his home country.

The child furnishes a dollhouse
with a spool table, wine cork stools,
a sardine can and its bathtub possibilities,
the content of her own construction.

*

Bachelard advances the theory
that any goal appears to be
in miniature, away on the horizon.

The girl continues, building a dresser
by stacking matchboxes
for drawers, with an ambition
already close enough to burning.

*

And the days on which nothing
is written, who will ever know
if they are of no note,

or the woman has come to
glory in tending to the need
of napkins to be put in rings, the feeding
of vases with the slim stems of flowers.

Brides come to the park
to be photographed,
late in life, against the backdrop
of borrowed flowers.

They've worked themselves
into white gowns. No matter
that they've wakened beside men
for years of rushed morning routines,

and are women as known
as the dresses displayed
days early in full light.

They lift the skirts above the dirt,
hugging their fabric to themselves.

&

Once I wore a white skirt, walking
with ice cream and a man.

It melted and spilled over
on my hem. He knelt

to suck out the stain.

And stopped there,
so, for years, the sense of his lips
has hovered on,

never lost in the lifting
of our layers of cover,

some sweaty
next unsubtlety.

            ⌒♭

The nights before ceremonies,
from my rental home, I can

see white tents raised, illuminated,
in the rose gardens.

And celebrate what has not
quite occurred, what could.

I walk out to the canopies
of what precedes.

Like a shave of palm sugar or the dash of Luxardo
in a cocktail, children's voices from the playground
are just a note in the air. That should be enough.
I wouldn't ask for a too-sweet, womanly drink.

One morning, I awoke after a blackout drunk
to find I'd done all the dishes. The miracle of the body
walks you where you ought to be though you won't recall,
then washes up from dinner. It could be
a kind of ideal: labor accomplished without awareness of it.

But I want that late hour in the kitchen back,
every hour, sloppy-staggering or soap-slick-clean.
Evening, with its lamps, is eager to be like early light,
and so often I have stayed until they meet.
Like lingering at a party to see last singles pair off. Or
being a wakeful mother waiting up. Must I choose?

Mornings, children stand waiting for the bus,
set out by each household as offerings to what will come.
Almost as if I could select one for my own. They are passive,
passengers preceding conveyance, nothing to do but stand
and be seen. And see.

Nothing expected but to stare at the neighbors' lots,
the walled gardens only inviting more investigation,
imagining a way through fence slats. To assess cracks
in sidewalks spread by roots. To ride the slight seesaws
of the loose cement pieces, watching your own feet.

How did I look, drunk? A condition acceptable
to speak of if I am sure to tell you I was younger then.
Not concerned with health, the long years ahead,

windows framing me, alone and unwholesome,
or homemaking, for whom? If anyone were looking.

In my life, I have made unusually much time for looking.

Let the children stand with their limbs hanging loose,
facing the street. They will soon be borne elsewhere.
By the aging body, into adult busyness, fuller hours.
Though how full are those hours? Haven't I
held my glass out whole nights, asking for more?

Reflective, skyscrapers
amplify the heat of the city,
bouncing the sun off their sides.
Walls I am in, where the cool
is plentiful and false. Phalanxes
of men running on gym machines
stay strong and go nowhere. Not a one
leaves. And because it does not rain,
the chalk drawings of children who play,
if they go outdoors, on cement,
are never erased and I live among
their summer instants as if
eternal. While store window displays
reassure that there is nothing wrong
with our growing numbers
and rising temperatures.
Red dress, red dress, red dress,
the warming world repeats,
racks well stocked with multiples.

It's called a *kneeling bus* because it lowers for those who need it.
And we bend our knees to allow others to pass. Here,
we're humble. The woman holding her briefcase the whole time
so it won't slip onto my side, the man mouthing every word
he reads but careful not to make a sound, each person
trying to fit some task into the bounds of their small seat
and hour, all diligence, drawn elbows, and dropped eyes.
There is not enough room to unfold the newspaper's
black headline (*Habitat Destruction*), but somehow, hope fits.
The others too, headed home, must look out the window
when we pass a building with a balloon tied to the mailbox.
Imagine that was your welcome. *You are wanted in this place.*
How often can humans feel less than harmful to where we are?
Balloons just outline the space occupied by the air
we would have expelled anyway, but they fill a room
with the promise of cake, sugar paste connecting one layer
to more of itself. Bus riders stack on board,
scanning for seats. There are open spaces, if only
in our searching eyes.

What becomes of the facts I learn and can't apply? (*Liming*
is spreading a paste on branches to capture birds.) Of words

about to be said before the bus starts or light turns
to red, flashing caution across the night?

Of the floral perfume confined in the buds of spring,
after a late frost's heavy covering? Of the wishes the married

woman will now never say? Of the feeling she possessed some
small beauty, gone with the inch of hair, trimmed too sensibly?

And the line cut for the sake of the larger poem?

But what if she'd spent the hours caring for hair, first impressions
yet to be made, or telling her same stories to a new person again,

drinking awkward drinks, then recovering? If either of the two
who make a house's singular scent took his old books or her cooking

elsewhere? If the road hadn't been abandoned before it reached
the building site, to be grown over, return to forest, as it should stay?

Don't I want hummingbirds to have flown safely away from nooses
of silk string collectors once hung from the necks of lilies?

Best that some things are left in disuse, lustrously dangling.

A dry river runs through,
or rather, idles in,

our small city where
we never intended to settle.

Between mudflats, on the few
pools, birds alight.

∽

We rinse glasses to be
filled with affordable whiskey,

with scotch or absinthe,
my love and I.

One swallow of good liquor
enough to scent the whole.

∽

A baptism in reverse—
that's birds in the river,

the bodies that enter
proclaiming the water pure.

They bow their heads. That is,
they dip their heads to drink.

∽

I no longer dream other lives,
forget other men.

He rubs the rims of Sazeracs
with rind. From the remains

of eaten fruit, makes
perfume arise.

When men end streams and make
artificial lakes, the bottoms

are blank and featureless
and so we sink crashed cars into them

to give fish a place to live.
I'd like to say that's beneficent.

And that ice melt, the sea rising,
will have a solution in it.

Imagine all the swimming then,
among wrecks filed along the freeways.

An idyll of engines stopped utterly.
No notion that a next life

above the one here
is ever to be had. Not even the halos

of opalescent motor oil
making the motion of ascending elsewhere.

Neighbors have erected an inflatable pumpkin
out of which arises an inflatable dog. Then
it descends, then rises again. I had imagined
a life set in another landscape, long stretches

of rivers and fields. Now I know it is autumn
from the lawn decorations, the lawn mowers
trimming the football field. Men measure
and spool out string, lay straight lines

of paint on the canvas they've been given,
the kind that keeps growing grass through
their accomplishments. Showing great care.
As I suppose they do padding and helmeting

five-year-old sons sent so soon to practice
struggle. Why not such a field as subject for study,
rather than a farm's, which was never pastoral
for many, not in the land of cotton, not for those

who hoed and picked it? And though the rivers here
are few, there is rain. When that water falls,
equally and indiscriminately soaking everyone's shoes,
it weights the inflatable dog. Now, nothing comes

from the pumpkin, and my love and I admit,
over our early supper, we are made earnestly sad.
We've got none of our young loftiness left,
nor laughter for others' losses, no matter their bad taste.

When the dog did work, its unfurling was slow,
one eye unfolding, a limb lengthening. It had done

this since September. A limb sagged out of sight,
an eye was sucked back, how many times already?

Yet we want all the measures, so much extension,
even of these days. Because the children on the field
rush forward. As bidden. Coaches screaming
that they can't cry. When they aren't. Five and already

they don't cry. They try for strong faces. People put up
what they'd like to look at. It doesn't stop them,
that the elements will take all ornament down.

On the human bodies of their gods,
Egyptians placed the heads
of falcon, lion, ibis, and jackal.

Mouths never contorted with words.
Give me a cat face. An inscrutability
so great as to be sublime.

After many years of *what I meant
to say* and *what I tried to show*, to whom
have I made reverence truly known?

Felines, mummified and gilded,
unchanged since ancient times,
wear the one expression

worth affixing in gold.

In museums, I have obeyed velvet cords' commands to keep my distance
from displays and stepped back farther still to get a better view of paintings.

But when I have gone to a hill above my home at night and watched
a well-known form (my mother, who will go on getting older,

or a man to whom I would make vows for life, which wouldn't be enough)
stepping away from a lit window, moving out of the frame—

I've wished that body would disregard whatever my words were
about wanting to walk alone, and would cross the dividing space,

bringing along its warm hands. That could blank my eyes from seeing
separations that will come. As it is with antique busts touched too much,

the paint of the pupils worn bare.

In the sun, I scorch,
dizzy. It's a *danger day*—
the new phrase for when being outdoors
can burn you dead.

And imagine: She'll have
her father's golden, resilient skin
(but my strong chin),
assembling a baby of best parts.

Shelley wrote *Frankenstein*
shivering, the Year Without Summer,
while volcanic ash encircled
the earth in shadow. Enwombed.

A sharp crust of frost covered all crops,
ruining corn in America, wrecking
Asia's rice fields. Farmers foraged
for nettles, then people ate clay, then they
themselves froze.

In this year's atmosphere—blazing
afternoons when laborers are warned
not to work, when children
may not play outside—

I also select words.
Try saying *nursery*,
not *unfurnished room*,
referring to the empty space
in our house, redeeming it.

Shelley salvaged
a few hundred pages, a great book,
from the tens of thousands
climate killed. And from her own body,
which had born another life, only briefly.
A child too soon entombed.

She warned against
the monsters humans can create,
and made her masterpiece.

As many women still try to do.
One strokes the round
of her stomach, sets her mind circling,
taking in swing sets and schools.
They are so near.

She extends the radius
of wishfulness
to the fantasy of a future,
in walking distance
widening out to
when my girl grows up.

Everything is past, below the overpass, behind in the speeding view, driving a six-lane, a straight, obliterating black line, interstate that can't be crossed, that cuts off animals car-struck, animals bone-cracked—I was about to say.

But I'd been to see the art of Nellie Mae, her *Pig on Expressway*, the pig biting his lip yet carrying his old figure forward into the fresh collision of colors. Her sculptures of chewed gum and marbles putting tired materials back into play. The drawings of butterfly dogs, donkey haints, women hens—hybrids adapted, hopes surviving. In purple pen on wallpaper, *Something That Ain't Been Born Yet*, a bushy-tailed, big-mouthed future life. And her letters in crayon command, "Can't turn around now, must get on the right road."

Litter flies in front of the windshield—a page printed with words. It was a book. It's become a bird, a just-begun breed, by being wind-tossed, by being torn to feathers. A right road? The cursive curve flows, somewhere for scrappier forms still to go.

(after Nellie Mae Rowe)

Crape myrtle's confetti of flowers.
Magnolia polished to mirror shine.
Live oaks that never will drop

their leaves, some standing since
the Civil War. And shacks,
empty of sharecroppers fled North.

Scenery of the South. Of survival.
For which trees still try. Seedling by seedling,
tree species can seek higher ground.

Can move, migrate where it's cooler
as the weather, one kind of climate, changes.
Many believe every *how it has always been*

will stay. While even rooted symbols,
to endure, edge away.

"Coywolf: New dog-coyote-wolf hybrid already numbers in the millions."

Out of coyote and wolf crossed. Out of coyote's compromises
about where to live, what to hunt. Out of wolf's big bones,
bearing wolf's bulk, fed by wolf's broad jaw, wolf's bite.

Out of dog, out of willingness to mate with dog,
out of tameness turned. Away from coyness. Out of coyness.

Into clamor, crashes of cars and construction, into noise
no longer weapon against the wild. Into crowds, into cities,
not creeping. Holding full tail high, nose proudly low
for the trails to where fat suburban rabbits go.

Into the unheralded havens of highway sides, into the unclaimed
kingdoms of park corners, into habitats we create
that cannot shelter us—the tender furless. Following graveyards'
green, beckoning glows from borough to borough. Each generation,
gorged on garbage, grows.

From earth, when we can no longer endure or
be endured. From cold forests cut and no more, from trees,
from all we've made fall like the trees. Following timber,
following trade routes, following trains, arriving by railroad,
as once to the West, another civilization—

Out of survival, out of desire for it, out of dogs past being pets
and the doggedness with which life persists
despite the end of one form. Out of the fresh tracks life lays.
Over the ways of we who will not scavenge
so cannot be saved. Street-crossing, side-walking,
coywolves, not coy, they come.

(after Philip Levine)

The graveyard gives the town its only green.
The graveyard, and the vacant lots.
Instead of dreaming houses to be built
on them, the possibility I could see
is of woods filling in again, returning.

And maybe I should have felt guilt once,
when I made love on the grass of a graveyard.
Though I was happy, lying there,
with our bodies, our living, and looking
up at the leaves.

Leaves have been what I wanted most,
on long walks in heat, when I kept moving forward
by thinking only, purely, of the next few trees,
a future that I'd fade into, fanned out as
shade.

ACKNOWLEDGMENTS

The author wishes to thank the following:

The publications in which many of these poems (often with different titles and in different forms) have appeared: *32 Poems*, *About Place Journal*, the Academy of American Poets website and *Poem-a-Day*, *Asheville Poetry Review*, *Birmingham Poetry Review*, *Catamaran Literary Reader*, *Construction*, *Ecotone*, *Fogged Clarity*, *Green Mountains Review*, the Jule Collins Smith Museum of Fine Art exhibit *Call and Response*, *The Kenyon Review*, the *Oxford American*, *Poetry Northwest*, *Prairie Schooner*, *The Southern Review*, *storySouth*, *The Swamp*, *Terrain.org*, *This Land*, *Tuesday: An Art Project*, and *Verse Daily*.

The sources from which I have gathered ideas, ranging from the *Radiolab* podcast episode "Super Cool" about Curzio Malaparte's book *Kaputt*, from which I have borrowed some of Walter Murch's language, to many literary texts such as David Ferry's translation of *The Georgics*, and from a number of writers whose commentaries on the *Oxford Junior Dictionary* preceded mine to the vocabulary and biology my parents taught me early, along with the ability to glean.

All the people and programs who have supported the writing of this book, including the Hambidge Center for the Creative Arts and Sciences, the MacDowell Colony, the Bread Loaf and Sewanee writers' conferences, the Frost Place, Auburn University's Department of English, Penguin Books and Paul in particular, Hannah (for fun and style, smarts and substance, and keeping me going in many senses), Anna, Maria, Derek, Austin, Ross, Deb, Gary, Lisa, Miriam, Laura-Gray, Laura, my parents (who deserve thanking again and again), and the one who has to live with the poems and poet every misstep of the way, my closest adviser and friend: Justin.

Rose McLarney's collections of poems are *Its Day Being Gone*, winner of the National Poetry Series, and *Forage*, both from Penguin Books, as well as *The Always Broken Plates of Mountains*, published by Four Way Books. She is coeditor of *A Literary Field Guide to Southern Appalachia* from University of Georgia Press. Rose has been awarded fellowships by the MacDowell Colony and the Bread Loaf and Sewanee writers' conferences; served as Dartmouth Poet in Residence at the Frost Place; and has received other prizes such as the Chaffin Award for Achievement in Appalachian Writing and the Fellowship of Southern Writers' George Garrett New Writing Award for Poetry. Her work has appeared in publications including *The Kenyon Review*, *The Southern Review*, *New England Review*, *Prairie Schooner*, *The Missouri Review*, the *Oxford American*, and many other journals. Rose earned her MFA from the MFA Program for Writers at Warren Wilson College and has taught at the college, among other institutions. Currently, she is associate professor of creative writing at Auburn University and coeditor in chief and poetry editor of the *Southern Humanities Review*.

PENGUIN POETS

PAIGE ACKERSON-KIELY
Dolefully, A Rampart Stands

JOHN ASHBERY
Selected Poems
Self-Portrait in a Convex Mirror

PAUL BEATTY
Joker, Joker, Deuce

JOSHUA BENNETT
The Sobbing School

TED BERRIGAN
The Sonnets

LAUREN BERRY
The Lifting Dress

JOE BONOMO
Installations

PHILIP BOOTH
Lifelines: Selected Poems 1950–1999
Selves

JIM CARROLL
Fear of Dreaming: The Selected Poems
Living at the Movies
Void of Course

ALISON HAWTHORNE DEMING
Genius Loci
Rope
Stairway to Heaven

CARL DENNIS
Another Reason
Callings
New and Selected Poems 1974–2004
Night School
Practical Gods
Ranking the Wishes
Unknown Friends

DIANE DI PRIMA
Loba

STUART DISCHELL
Backwards Days
Dig Safe

STEPHEN DOBYNS
Velocities: New and Selected Poems: 1966–1992

EDWARD DORN
Way More West

ROGER FANNING
The Middle Ages

ADAM FOULDS
The Broken Word

CARRIE FOUNTAIN
Burn Lake
Instant Winner

AMY GERSTLER
Crown of Weeds
Dearest Creature
Ghost Girl
Medicine
Nerve Storm
Scattered at Sea

EUGENE GLORIA
Drivers at the Short-Time Motel
Hoodlum Birds
My Favorite Warlord
Sightseer in This Killing City

DEBORA GREGER
By Herself
Desert Fathers, Uranium Daughters
God
In Darwin's Room
Men, Women, and Ghosts
Western Art

TERRANCE HAYES
American Sonnets for My Past and Future Assassin
Hip Logic
How to Be Drawn
Lighthead
Wind in a Box

NATHAN HOKS
The Narrow Circle

ROBERT HUNTER
Sentinel and Other Poems

MARY KARR
Viper Rum

WILLIAM KECKLER
Sanskrit of the Body

JACK KEROUAC
Book of Blues
Book of Haikus
Book of Sketches

JOANNA KLINK
Circadian
Excerpts from a Secret Prophecy
Raptus

JOANNE KYGER
As Ever: Selected Poems

ANN LAUTERBACH
Hum
If in Time: Selected Poems, 1975–2000
On a Stair
Or to Begin Again
Spell
Under the Sign

CORINNE LEE
Plenty
Pyx

PHILLIS LEVIN
May Day
Mercury
Mr. Memory & Other Poems

PATRICIA LOCKWOOD
Motherland Fatherland Homelandsexuals

WILLIAM LOGAN
Macbeth in Venice
Madame X
Rift of Light
Strange Flesh
The Whispering Gallery

J. MICHAEL MARTINEZ
Museum of the Americas

ADRIAN MATEJKA
The Big Smoke
Map to the Stars
Mixology

MICHAEL MCCLURE
Huge Dreams: San Francisco and Beat Poems

ROSE MCLARNEY
Forage
Its Day Being Gone

DAVID MELTZER
David's Copy: The Selected Poems of David Meltzer

ROBERT MORGAN
Dark Energy
Terroir

CAROL MUSKE-DUKES
Blue Rose
An Octave Above Thunder
Red Trousseau
Twin Cities

ALICE NOTLEY
Certain Magical Acts
Culture of One
The Descent of Alette
Disobedience
In the Pines
Mysteries of Small Houses

WILLIE PERDOMO
The Crazy Bunch
The Essential Hits of Shorty Bon Bon

DANIEL POPPICK
Fear of Description

LIA PURPURA
It Shouldn't Have Been Beautiful

LAWRENCE RAAB
The History of Forgetting
Visible Signs

BARBARA RAS
The Last Skin
One Hidden Stuff

MICHAEL ROBBINS
Alien vs. Predator
The Second Sex

PATTIANN ROGERS
Generations
Holy Heathen Rhapsody
Quickening Fields
Wayfare

SAM SAX
Madness

ROBYN SCHIFF
A Woman of Property

WILLIAM STOBB
Absentia
Nervous Systems

TRYFON TOLIDES
An Almost Pure Empty Walking

SARAH VAP
Viability

ANNE WALDMAN
Gossamurmur
Kill or Cure
Manatee/Humanity
Structure of the World Compared to a Bubble
Trickster Feminism

JAMES WELCH
Riding the Earthboy 40

PHILIP WHALEN
Overtime: Selected Poems

ROBERT WRIGLEY
Anatomy of Melancholy and Other Poems
Beautiful Country
Box
Earthly Meditations: New and Selected Poems
Lives of the Animals
Reign of Snakes

MARK YAKICH
The Importance of Peeling Potatoes in Ukraine
Spiritual Exercises
Unrelated Individuals Forming a Group Waiting to Cross